THE NATIONAL POETRY SERIES

The National Poetry Series was established in 1978 to publish five books of poems annually through participating trade publishers. Publication of these books is funded by James A. Michener, Edward J. Piszek, the Ford Foundation, the Witter Bynner Foundation, and the publishers—Doubleday; E. P. Dutton; Harper & Row; Holt, Rinehart and Winston; Random House.

THE NATIONAL POETRY SERIES—1982

Jonathan Aaron, SECOND SIGHT *(Selected by Anthony Hecht)*
Cyrus Cassells, THE MUD ACTOR *(Selected by Al Young)*
Denis Johnson, THE INCOGNITO LOUNGE *(Selected by Mark Strand)*
Naomi Shihab Nye, HUGGING THE JUKEBOX *(Selected by Josephine Miles)*
Sherod Santos, ALL THE SAD ETCETERA *(Selected by Charles Wright)*

SECOND SIGHT

Poems by
JONATHAN AARON

Winner of the Open Competition
The National Poetry Series

Selected by ANTHONY HECHT

HARPER & ROW, PUBLISHERS, New York
Cambridge, Philadelphia, San Francisco, London
Mexico City, São Paulo, Sydney

1817

My thanks to the Yaddo Corporation for giving me time to finish a number of these poems.

—J.A.

Some of the poems in this collection have appeared in the following publications in slightly different form: *The Iowa Review, Kayak, The New Yorker, Ploughshares,* and *The Yale Review.*

"Going Away" originally appeared in *American Review #21,* October 1974, published by Bantam Books, Inc. Copyright © 1974 by Jonathan Aaron.

"Nothing to Be Afraid Of" is a translation of *"Rien à craindre,"* from *Histoires* by Jacques Prévert. © Editions Gallimard, 1963.

"From a Doorway" originally appeared in the December 1971 issue of *Esquire* under the title "Introduction to the Sleepers."

Italicized lines on page 60 from "The Viper" by Nicanor Parra, translated from the Spanish by Miller Williams, are from *Poems and Anti-Poems* by Nicanor Parra. Copyright © 1967 by New Directions Publishing Corporation. Reprinted by permission of New Directions Publishing Corporation and Laurence Pollinger Ltd.

SECOND SIGHT. Copyright © 1982 by Jonathan Aaron. All rights reserved. Printed in the United States of America. No part of this book may be used or reproduced in any manner whatsoever without written permission except in the case of brief quotations embodied in critical articles and reviews. For information address Harper & Row, Publishers, Inc., 10 East 53rd Street, New York, N.Y. 10022. Published simultaneously in Canada by Fitzhenry & Whiteside Limited, Toronto.

FIRST EDITION

Designer: Sidney Feinberg

Library of Congress Cataloging in Publication Data

Aaron, Jonathan.
  Second sight.
  (The National Poetry series)
    I. Hecht, Anthony, 1923– . II. Title. III. Series.
PS3551.A7S4   1982   811'.54   81-48026
                                   AACR2
ISBN 0-06-014969-8   82 83 84 85 86 10 9 8 7 6 5 4 3 2 1
ISBN 0-06-090944-7 (pbk.)   82 83 84 85 86 10 9 8 7 6 5 4 3 2 1

for David
and for Rebecca

Contents

9   *Introduction*

I
13 Little Memoir
15 Farther Away
17 The Foreigner
19 Finding the Landscape
20 The Other Passengers
23 Stray Dog
25 Cooking an Omelette
27 Memories of the Dictator
30 Nothing to Be Afraid Of
32 Consequences of a Dime
35 Guests
37 The Hydrant

II
41 Natural Things
43 The Spell
46 Meeting Like This
48 Meanwhile
49 Somebody Else for a Change

III

- 57 Second Sight
- 60 Here Everything Is Still Floating
- 62 From a Doorway
- 63 Betty & John
- 65 Bonnard's Wife
- 66 Putting It Mildly
- 67 Going Away
- 69 What It Was Like There
- 70 Where You Were Going
- 72 Preparations
- 75 Auras
- 77 The Ribbons
- 78 The Summons

Introduction

> Two theories of poetry. Poetry as a magical means for inducing desirable emotions and repelling undesirable emotions in oneself and others, or Poetry as a game of knowledge, a bringing to consciousness, by naming them, of emotions and their hidden relationships. The first view was held by the Greeks, and is now held by MGM, Agit-Prop, and the collective public of the world. They are wrong.
> —W. H. AUDEN

> History, Stephen said, is a nightmare from which I am trying to awake.
> —JAMES JOYCE

Here is a splendid, lively and daring book; lovely but tricky, so prepare to be charmed and puzzled. Some of Jonathan Aaron's poems are intimate, amused and amusing; nearly, so it seems, casual. But by the time you reach their end you're aware of a certain edginess, a *frisson* of not unpleasurable fear; such as perhaps might be aroused by a roller coaster, an amusement fair's fun house, Mme. Tussaud's waxworks or a *Grand Guignol* performance. These poems exhibit a curious, slippery teetering between comedy and grief. They are full of sly ventures into the forbidden or the dangerous, they resonate with innuendos of the uncanny, and they summon from some abyss or other a mixture of sensations the more puzzling for being disconcertingly familiar.

And now, unsettled and alert, we move into poems that candidly employ the vocabulary of crime, the furniture of detective fiction, with its promises of grotesque revelations. One masterly presence behind the poet may indeed be Edgar Allan Poe, whose narrators seem to wish to bring to bear every force of rationality to confront and explain what appears to be inexplicable. In the words of the title poem, "... At first I was convinced/the secret of these episodes/ lay ... For that matter,/I felt sure ... True, there was/evidence to the contrary ..." But of course it is not

Poe of which we are primarily reminded, nor is Mr. Aaron simply borrowing the conventions of another genre. The poems are constantly asking us, as much by their silences as by their words, to "investigate" what it is precisely they remind us of; and I would tentatively suggest that they resemble two quite distinct and supposedly separate parishes of the soul.

The first of these is that putative "real world" in which (a) a young man eager to impress a movie star who happens to be a Yale freshman shoots the President of the United States, (b) a fanatical, patriotic Turk, claiming to protest the foreign policies of the United States and the Soviet Union, shoots the Pope, (c) hijackers and terrorists, in order to secure their effects, must select victims who are precisely blameless, and (d) another President of the United States, in Oval-Office consultation with his most intimate aides, considers employing union thugs and professional killers to "punish" those who are peacefully demonstrating in behalf of peace.

In thinking of these instances (and the list is shockingly extensible) one is struck by how much they resemble the characteristic dramas of that other, interior and private parish that belongs to the world of dream and fable and the vast unconscious *terra incognita*. Mr. Aaron's Dictator, for example, may well be the tyrannous Conscious Mind, nervously aware of the constant danger of underground subversion and insurrection. In this alternate parish you are forever seeking for clues ". . . to help you interpret a message/sleep delivers in code." Mr. Aaron's poetry will not allow us to forget how precarious is our grip on what we fancy to be the solidities of our existence. And so his poems, like our dreams, are full of a mysterious pertinence. And a poignant loneliness. But in defiance of all laws, physical, logical and political, they stand before us as vivid instances of *second sight*.

—Anthony Hecht

I

> The person we look at, or who feels he is being looked at, looks at us in turn. To perceive the aura of an object we look at means to invest it with the ability to look at us in return.
>
> —WALTER BENJAMIN

Little Memoir

Finally I got to Paris,
city of little miracles,
where, on a diet of snails
and duck, I completely recovered
from the terrible disaster
of the Moscow Competition.
Still, it was November,
clouds ragged and confused
among the filthy buttresses
of Notre-Dame. I went to parties
to persuade myself it was useless
preparing for emergencies,
but people kept talking about
the season's emptiness,
the weather's delay. So
I returned to my apartment,
sold everything, and listened.
Soon I heard a knock on the door.
An important childhood friend
stood at the threshold.
Years before she'd taught me
to read my palm in a mirror,
taught me travel as a means
of slowing down the future—
the sound of approaching footsteps
as proof that I am, for certain
short periods, invisible.
I looked out the half-open window

at the park across the street,
where evening had already dropped
its net beneath the trees,
saw a blue light tremble
in the leaves of the nearest
chestnut. I was about to speak
when she held up her hand
for a moment's silence in honor,
I thought, of special circumstances
gathering to declare themselves
at last. A cold draft
was pulling at the tropical beach
scene I'd torn from a magazine
and pinned up by the phone.

Farther Away

It could be early in the morning,
the sky so young
you think you see
ash rising
from the smokeless stack
of the power plant.
Or it could be five minutes
to three in the afternoon,
the sun's angle a lie,
the piazza deserted
because of more
in the air than the pennants
snapping above the town hall's
intricate crenelations.
Or maybe it is still
the middle of the night,
day the effect
of some celestial accident
quietly taking place
on the other side
of the railroad station.
Pausing in the sudden shadow
of the war memorial,
we think better of calling.
Who would rouse
an unknown townspeople
from its sleep,
or the dead from theirs,
if he could help it?

Our train appears
a last time, toylike, funereal,
beyond the wheatfields.
We hear its delicate whistle
farther and farther away.

The Foreigner

When I wake up, the game is already over.
The dusky city is full of people out of their minds
with disappointment, fat people eating pizza,
thin people whose only remaining ambition
is to gain weight or die. Inside the stadium
fans are still attacking the goal posts
like antibodies. The restaurant I enter is crowded
with the sound of quiet weeping, for now
that the season is over and the championship settled
forever, all that's left is the sweet sorrow
of eating. The new mayor himself is a dietitian.
Moments after his inauguration, I hear him
explain why his first official act will be to move
his family into a house carved from a gigantic onion.
I've never felt better in my life! he announces
from his half-peeled doorstep, his face shining
with tears. Everyone keeps quiet, expecting the words
Health and *Victory* to appear in black ink
above the neighboring woods. But soon my eyes start watering
when the wind shifts. My fingers itch for something more
to hold on to than a vegetable. The next thing I know
I'm standing on a promontory overlooking the harbor.
From here I can see the entire city,
hear its traffic like someone's breath
in a dark room. I figure I can reach the water
in less than ten minutes by running fast enough.

It's true, swimming away from all this is another problem,
but it's better than listening to the empty corrections
of the crowds, better than arguing the scores fixed
in the new almanacs, better than bearing the present
into a future that has already happened.

Finding the Landscape

Last night you questioned the number of stars
on your index finger. Their replies were guarded,
nameless. Now, above the mist, cold planets

linger to help you interpret a message
sleep delivered in code. You read it
with your eyes closed and discover the cities

behind you are empty, the people sealed
and silent in their breathing rooms.
You stop reading and listen to a robin

sing like a drink of water. You know
there is salvation in the eye of the moment,
and coming to yourself in a tree's glitter

at half-light, you settle for it.
But the landscape is lying on its side, so you
lie down on your side to see, your assumptions

rolling from your pockets into the black acres
past the beach. Seaward, beyond anything
you expected, there are no sails, only

a glimpse of the stars you relied on shaking
into laminated darkness like fish, and the horizon
sweeping your eyes with its little white flag.

The Other Passengers

As we drop from the rainy north
the sky clears. Gardens
flow past. Billows of oak
and pine change to shining
rectangles of wheat.

The other passengers
stare out their windows,
given to gusts
of inquiry or exclamation,
dark-eyed men and women,
their baggage everywhere,
suitcases lashed with twine,
packages wrapped in newspaper,
plastic satchels full of bread,
oranges, bottles of wine.

We follow
the curves of a muddy river
into their country.
The tracks tilt us over
the water. A constant wall
of trees on the far bank
rolls backward at a speed
that seems to leave us
going nowhere. Someone
switches on a radio—static
and snatches of high,
unsteady singing.

The air is warm
and close,
and I begin suspecting
I forgot something
in my hotel room. Once more
I'm climbing the narrow,
carpeted stairs, pausing
before a door that opens
as I reach for it,
and step into
the shaded air.

Here's the ill-lit
line of dancers,
music, smoke. Here's
the fat man in a white suit,
who says he knows life
like the back of his hand,
who says, lighting a cigar,
*Even though I'm more
the way I used to be than you
can imagine, I've changed
and hold nothing against you.*

Again I try to relax
amid the rising clamor
of an argument, laughter,
the orchestra. And again
the woman beside me
takes off her glasses.
Where have you been? I ask,
still in the dark.
What happened?

It's a long story,
she begins.

We slow
past houses, roofs
black against the low sun,
some sort of town.
A man across the aisle
holds an apple in one hand,
a jackknife in the other. Two women
who could be younger than they look
stand up, their eyes hidden
in the shadows of their shawls.

They are talking,
but the sound of their voices
is the sound of the radio,
songs I can't understand,
others I've been trying to recall,
the pulse of the wheels
carrying each of us along
the arc of what would become
a perfect circle
if we had time
to travel that far.

Stray Dog

While he jogs
head-down toward
the memory of a taste,
a voice, a moment
of doorway,

his front legs
constantly fail
to correct his hindquarters'
sleepy need to travel
somewhere else.

Only his narrow,
low-slung muzzle
gives the rest of him
reason to follow.

His skin
is a thin blanket
thrown over the old argument
of his skeleton
to keep the rain out
and the dry guts in.

Each step he takes
is an achievement
of what remains
ready at any moment
to become less
than the sum of its parts.

But whenever paw hits
pavement, the shock
ripples down or up his knobby
spine, his bones are shaken
into cooperation,

and all of him
settles into motion
continuous as the
twist of water
in the gutter beside him.

Ready to cross the wet street,
he glances at the traffic,
eyes glowing
zeroes, neon and fathomless
before they dim
into a green of sea-worn glass
as he looks the other way.

Cooking an Omelette

Break two eggs
into a large bowl, preferably
a blue one.
Look down and see
them staring back at you,
their innocent embrace
affirming what must happen.
Now add salt (kosher salt is best,
being saltiest),
pepper, parsley (fresh-
snipped with scissors)
to remind you of the woods you'd like
to be in, a few flakes
of oregano, and
a backhand pinch of thyme,
which tells you you are cooking.

Tilt the bowl to favor gravity
and with a whisk
whip it all into a froth, a midget
ecosystem of delight.
You may here wish to remember
the perfect symmetry of childhood
mornings. Set
your dented, seasoned frying pan
with a light clang
over a high flame,
and drop a pat of butter in.
Wait until the pan is shining

with dark heat, then lower the flame.
Pour your mixture into the pan, and listen.
The hiss is a reward.

Jog the pan in brief, determined arcs
above the flame to flounce the yellow foam
in waves against the hot wall of the pan.
When little is left to riffle outward from
the center, strike the pan at the handle's base
with the butt-end of a spatula or knife
to loosen what you've made from the clinging metal.
Fold the settled, slightly moistened roundness gently
over toward the far side of the pan to create
a *lozenge-of-egg*.
Roll it from the canted pan
onto a white plate.

If you've cooked it for your sweetie—
she having just arrived to find there's nothing
in the house—you might want to please her
further by tossing on some more chopped herbs for color.
If it's for yourself, forgo
such niceties, which only
measure solitude. Pick it up
with both hands and begin.

Memories of the Dictator

1
Sleeping with somebody, he'd use
the *bel canto* technique, which was
difficult, he said, but very beautiful.
He took care of himself—watched
what he ate, got plenty of rest.
Sometimes he took a cure.

His tastes were simple.
Four or five cigarettes
over a *National Geographic*.
Children's stories for
that warm feeling of the shoes
filling up with nostalgia.

Remember the old lady who left
her vital organs to her cat?
Or the disappointed heart surgeon
who ate the aneurysm?
What you have heard may be true,
and this is where he comes in.

2
Understand, he knew nothing
before he discovered that the
ballistic properties of memory
were what kept him falling
toward his fondest target—

to become anything you needed,
wanted to afford, or thought
you should die for.

Millions loved the exoticism
of his law of personal gravity,
but finally observers began
to report that "camouflage"
wasn't the right term for explaining
the disappearance of the man
who resembled him like a brother.

3
For twenty years of bad nights
he'd dream his commands
were extended slips of the tongue.
Each morning he'd make a list
of his latest insights,
writing them down on his clothes,
stray envelopes, tables and chairs.
And finding he still couldn't read them
he'd offer huge rewards
to any hammer-brain who could manage
to break down wind-code,
star-code, cloud-code.

4
He tried to keep calm throughout
a life of periodic terrors, hoping
the first time for anything
was really the second, but in one

of his late diaries he suspects
that being a genius is like
being married to a troll
and starving to death. Pain
stopped minding its own business
in his chest. An international team
of doctors argued and published
disorderly theories. The colonels
stopped talking. His shadow trailed
a rope only he could see.

5
Few will discuss it now,
but more and more believe
in his return. They say
he will come to himself some evening
in his special graveyard, convinced
he didn't go far enough. A man in sunglasses
and a white suit will get out of a cab
at the edge of the capital and enter
a restaurant. "When was the last time
you saw him alive?" he will cry out.
"What's all this about
a fire? Who said anything
about a corpse in the ashes?"
And everyone will stop eating,
unable to remember the answers.

Nothing to Be Afraid Of

(after Jacques Prévert)

Don't be afraid
Good people
There's no danger
The dead are quite dead
They're well shut away
There's nothing to be afraid of
Nobody can take them from you
They themselves can't get away
There are guards in the cemeteries
And what's more
Around every grave
There's an iron fence
Like the bars of the cribs
In which the littlest children are sleeping

A wise precaution
After all
You never know
Deep in its last sleep
A corpse could still dream
Dream it's no longer a corpse
Dream it's alive
And throwing aside its stone bedclothes
Free itself
Lean out
A catacomb horror
Tumble from the tomb
Like a child from bed
Back into life

It's easy to picture
And everything would fall back into question
Affection grief
Who gets what from the will

But cheer up
Good people
You don't have to worry
The dead will not return
To enjoy themselves on earth
You shed your tears once and for all
And you will never ever
Have to discuss it again
Nothing in the cemetery
Will be uprooted
The pots of chrysanthemums
Will stay right where they are
And in front of the mausoleum
Watering can in hand
You will be free to devote yourselves
In total tranquillity
To cultivating your little plots
Of eternal regret

Consequences of a Dime

I deposit a dime
and prepare to keep calm, remembering rage—
which grows like a weed in these conditions,
making the eyes water

and the hands shake—
can keep me from calling at all. To assure
each digit I dial I keep my finger in
the recoiling spindle.

I can feel its coarse
reluctance as I read the attempts of others
scored with penknife, car key, scissors. They
have come and gone,

but I am here.
Each rasp in my ear has its own color, each
darker than the last, deepening finally into
a vascular purple which

shoves new slugs of itself
ahead into silence. A hoarse voice answers.
Perhaps it has a white face, large smoked
teeth, a hairless head.

It says it hasn't
had anything to eat in days. Its pockets are
large and empty, it has a can opener
but no can to open.

But self-restraint
is a matter of discipline, it explains.
It has been instructed not to reveal
the whereabouts of B,

and disobeying orders
would mean its job, its life. I argue
for information. What job? What life?
Comfortable stone houses

crowd the corniches,
the voice concedes gloomily, and
the weather is Caribbean. It quotes prices
and the names of lawyers,

bankers and real estate
agents. Which is the most desirable location
on the cliffs? I ask, and it tells me
the northernmost promontory

is already leased
to a Lebanese businessman named Hakim,
who has a new wife, a beautiful, reclusive
soprano from Milan.

I'm getting the picture—
sunlight and armed guards, limousines nose
to nose in the shadow of a dusty villa,
when the voice laughs

like someone late
getting a joke. You should see yourself! it says,

suddenly breathless. Stuck in a phone booth
and a hundred miles

colder than this morning!
Look around. Is there enough light left
for you to make your next mistake?
Static and the dial tone

rise and thicken
in my head like all my recent attempts
to say goodbye. I hammer the cradle
with the receiver

hoping to break something.
Then I hang up and welcome the quiet until
I notice a man walking toward me smiling,
holding out his hands.

Guests

This morning out on the fairgrounds
they found the footprints, the same ones
I described to the Professor

the night he disappeared.
I recall his departure as clearly
as if I'd wanted it to happen.

There had been rain for a week.
He followed the winding path
from the house through the pines

down to the lake while everyone else
stayed inside playing bridge
and arguing about bird migrations.

Later I refused to answer questions.
I knew I had to think of something—
a witness, another codicil,

whatever tightened in my head
when the house started filling up
with strangers, drinking

and dancing, crazy parties.
I couldn't stand it, so I finally
locked myself in the library,

turned off the lights.
For hours I stood at the window
trying to imagine how long

it takes to travel to the great
nerve centers of the world. And
the sunset persisted, as if

waiting for the right moment
to illuminate the facts from which
I am always about to awaken.

The Hydrant

Only one exists.
Its unimaginable speed
obviates the need for others.
In fact, though nothing could act
less disposed to move,
have less an air
of imminence about it, the hydrant
is the world's sole figment
of what ought to be called
the state of absolute
motion, or the principle of being
everywhere at once.
Its nature is constant,
instantaneous transit.
When you see two, three, more,
near and farther along
some eventless neighborhood prospect,
it is the hydrant
in full oscillation, seeming many
through a series of lightning
shifts from one spot
to others. When night
is torn open by a white fierceness
which the silhouettes of firefighters
look arranged against, as in
the classic tabloid
photograph, the hydrant
is always near enough to water
to sustain its appearances: that squat nubbin,

red, yellow, or black,
newly installed,
or rusted, grass-choked, on its side
in front of a tenement
slated for demolition—
that thumb with warts on it
down there on the corner nearest your house.
But who could have known
the hydrant is swiftly
and forever so alone?
Whoever took the time
to look twice and question
its regardless immobility?
We see what we want to see,
or what some system
for which there is no longer,
or not yet, a term
fitting our whereabouts, wants
us to believe. And who can tell
how many other objects we depend on
also have minds of their own,
their own methods of concealment, are also
reasons why we know things
are never as they seem?

II

> Behind everything there is always
> The unknown unwanted life.
>
> —RANDALL JARRELL

Natural Things

Large and small excited girls
are holding things
that look like pruning hooks
or tuning forks—a parody
of the craze for clubs and rhythm
which grips the younger generation
during any time of crisis.

Those with round heads
are dominant, even when
they walk on their hands
toward a hole in the middle
of their exercise yard. (This is
more a mirage than stereometry.)
They collect like water around the earth's ankles.
They rise when they hear the moon
squeal on its hinges.

Those with square heads
lean toward death
as an experiment in technique.
They accept there is no vanishing
point beyond a doubt of life's
basic questions, *e.g.*,
When? Where? How much?

Then there is the possibility
this is all a game. The girls wake up
Saturdays playing the piano.

Their teacher, a bearded ornithologist
who needs the money, clears his throat
on the afternoon of their first recital
and declares:

"Don't forget! Goethe and Klee
each loved natural things and owned
an herbarium and a small collection of mice,
seaweed and stones which they kept nicely
displayed in their studios!"

The Spell

The witch is dancing
for the bride and groom
in iron shoes
red-hot and heavier than doorstops.
Her former servants
wager on how long she'll last,
then in rough chorus count
each step she manages until her eyes
roll up and she waves her arms
in a final, ridiculous effort to fly.
Hand in hand with her lucky
simpleton, the princess
hovers in the charmed air, nodding
and smiling on the sacrifice.
Her new dress could have been made
from the petals of those huge
white flowers which so frightened her
years ago in the forest.
They glowed like faces in the dark
and called her by her name.
Now she is
her own source of light, an intricate,
bell-shaped lamp ascending of its own
accord into a likelihood
no one looking up at her can calculate.
The guests are shouting
and knocking each other down
trying to see better. Some put on
animal masks and dance on the tables,

scattering what's left of the buffet.
In a far corner six pale musicians
sit at attention with their eyes closed.
The seventh keeps clubbing his drum
to a rhythm that struggles
not to come back to him.
It occurs to me I can't remember
the magic word for wakefulness, or uncle,
and a man with a fox's face
appears beside me, smelling of barnyard,
a few feathers stuck to his muzzle,
picking his teeth
with a chicken bone. He says
something in German and jabs
a paw in the direction
of the royal pair already small
and drifting in shreds of luminous blue
cloud near the topmost arches
of the hall. Suddenly every one of us
breathes in deeply
at the same moment. But whoever is
walking over my grave
takes his time:
late-afternoon sunlight splays
through the clover-leaf mullions
behind me and wanders
over tapestry and stone
wall like the fingers of a blind man's hand.
Outside and seemingly far away
a dog's barking sounds like someone
hammering nails.
Then a plate hits the floor
with a solitary clang

that echoes in a narrowing funnel of alarm.
The spell falters, the raucous milling
breaks back on us from silence
and a faint memory of better judgment.
And as gusts of applause rise
from the crowd toward the new
inhabitants of guesswork and altitude,
the fox resumes his story in my ear,
this time, in spite of his accent,
talking my language.

Meeting Like This

Today at the chemist's
your husband bought
another bottle
of formaldehyde,
and now he's downstairs

singing "Mansions
of Death," the hymn,
so you know
we can't go on
meeting like this.

Haven't you guessed
why the air
so strangely emptied
of sound
the last time you began

undressing? It was him,
wherever he was,
absorbing the echo
of your shawl's latest
accumulation

on the floor.
Forgive me.
This isn't really
what I'd planned on
happening.

If only we could go
to America,
where there are no
nightingales.
I don't even have to close

my eyes to see us
in some hotel
named for a President
no one remembers,
a place filled

with soft, untraceable
music and the ageless
calm of being
nowhere anyone
could die. Dowagers

and their wards
float in the icy light
of chandeliers.
Unable to sleep
we find ourselves

an abandoned ballroom.
A little wind
murmurs in the rafters.
Stars signal
through a hole in the roof.

Meanwhile

The Commander keeps opening and shutting windows,
making sure some doors are locked and others
properly ajar. He insists on sitting only
in chairs which give him a good view of all the approaches
to the room he's in. He has dinner
in the conservatory. Afterward
there is always silence, and with moonlight
the persistent hurt it took him years
to learn to live with prompting him
to look under a corner of a rug
or seize a book from a shelf in the library
and shake it frantically.
"Someone must have eaten it," he sighs,
"or else none of this ever happened
in my lifetime." He has come to believe
in the force of what is missing.
When he shuffles cards, they lie down slowly on the table.
It is a long time from being hungry
to deciding to eat. The words keep coming
back to him: *Blue sky. Blue sky.*
In the throat of a large rock in the garden,
fresh water listens.

Somebody Else for a Change

> ... And when she went in she recognized
> Snow-white; and she stood still with
> rage and fear, and could not stir.

1
Then the crowd turned ugly
and took her presence into its own
rough hands. The bride and groom
couldn't bear to scrutinize the smoky
uproar and kept out of it
discussing their honeymoon, never dreaming
her burns and broken bones only
looked that way. Her iron shoes
were a size too small, she had
no music to dance to, but it was
simpler than saying goodbye,
she reasoned, stepping into shadow
right on schedule, leaving nothing
to fate but her laboratory and a lost
appetite for the occult. And well
before the festival had begun
to pall into the proverbial
rainy morning after, she was far away,
soaking her aches in a hot bath
and savoring being somebody else
for a change. She thought of her step-
daughter, the new Queen, and didn't
envy her a thing. On the contrary,
she felt as if a great stone
had just been lifted from her heart.

2
Now she could forget the way
any day rises and falls no matter how
much you might wish it were otherwise,
deal herself solitaire, listen
to songs on a little crank-powered
victrola, like the records she played
a present from the future, salvaged
and offered her once upon a time
by a sentimental familiar. Melodies
of gently deliberate irresolution
made her yearn for someone to forgive.
At night, in the depths of sleep, she gazed
at the ocean from a grassy
slope that made her feel vaguely
off-balance, or sat at a gaming table
counting bills of endlessly varying
denominations. So she planned a journey,
poring over maps of places she had
never heard of, strangely drawn along
red veins of road, through soft greens
of forest and yellows of desert, toward
the nameless grey beyond her story's edge.

3
She sampled the ritual of one
coastal casino after another, but even
before they were dealt, the cards
would confess everything—for the sake of
old acquaintance, they declared,
or in honor of all those fortunes told
in the interests of a criminal science.

To scramble their chatter, she memorized
numbers she wrote on small squares
of paper and then picked out of a hat
blindfolded. She would start arguing
with the nearest stranger the moment
she heard the subtle statements of intention
material objects tend to issue when
large sums come into question. Finally
she took refuge in a modest villa
overlooking one of the less fashionable
Italian lakes. From her terrace she observed
the cloud-wrack speeding south through
a confusion of local Alps, the sky
a menagerie of forms she had not forgotten.

4
Light was discovered to be a wave.
The kinetic theory of gases spread
through the civilized world like a slow
fire. Angels found it pointless dancing
on the head of a pin. All the same,
crop failures continued, people disappearing
in the woods, and the Queen and King oblivious
in an atmosphere of deepening somnolence.
The palace had long since become a spa
full of serious-looking people who lived
on mineral water and softly personal inquiries
about weight loss and humor level. Whenever
anyone happened to report a different sort
of problem—blood, for instance,
welling from the large, etiolated onions
cook would chop for soups, or a bell

where there was no bell ringing and ringing
just before dawn—court philosophers
would dismiss it as a lingering aspect
of some outdated fact easily accounted for
by last week's changes in the weather.

5
Walking at the edge of her lake
one afternoon, she noticed movement
just below the water's surface.
A human shape, transparent, almost
invisible, nosed the shallows
at her feet. "Talk to me," she said,
not feeling very good about this
obvious concession to a principle
she had washed her hands of,
but wanting advice. *But you never listen,*
she heard, as if through a shut door.
The lake looked enormous. The nearby
mountains leaned in her direction. She
hung on. "What have I overlooked?"
A long pause. Then: *You know
how carelessness is its own reward, like
wishful thinking or an educated guess?
Keep trying to calculate the distances
between now and who you were,
and you'll wake up out there, beyond
shouting range, sitting in a small boat
with a hole in it.* A wind rose, scuffing
the freezing water. The shape shrugged
and burst apart in an instant
like a school of fish.

6
Sooner or later, at a dull reception,
the royal couple fell
into conversation with a woman
dressed in one of the traditional holiday
costumes of the region. Her hair silver,
her complexion becomingly pale, she was,
to those who might have remembered,
unrecognizable. "Live long, learn long,"
she assured them, holding up her empty hands
and smiling, her words elusive, musical,
a touch of fresh air in an untrimmed rosebush.
Of course, they liked her
so much they asked her to be
godmother to their three children, who,
upon being introduced, pelted her
with questions such as: Can fish talk?
Is the air alive? What do you see
when you close your eyes that way?

7
But that evening, when the children
asked her for the story ending
with a big wedding where the old lady dances
herself to death because she has to,
she felt dizzy, hot and cold,
unpleasantly short of
breath. "It never happened," she said,
in spite of herself. We know
what we know! they chorused back. The mirror
was a portrait of her conscience!
The apple was a taste of her heart! *Fresh air,*

she thought and reached for the nearest
window. Whereupon the little light
a sunset leaves in any pane of glass
turned into something she hadn't seen
in years, a woman's face sketchily
afloat in the abiding glow of jealousy
and scientific will. The children waited.
As she looked into her own eyes
forgotten spells and intuitions
started coming back to her in a
ragged clamor, demanding utterance.

III

He never disappears from view because there are no perspectives.
—ZBIGNIEW HERBERT

Second Sight

I could never tell
when that peculiar drowsiness
would steal over her.
The light would dim and the window
rattle as if to rain
or a handful of pebbles.
The ocean's expectant hush
would fill the room. Then
she would simply go under
and in someone else's voice
start reciting the least lessons
of weather, or the ways north
changes south of our experience.
At first I was convinced
the secret of these episodes
lay at the heart of a time-
and-motion study I'd planned
to conduct on a series of night
drives through her home town
with my ears wide open
and a microphone. For that matter,
I felt sure the primrose blossoms
collaring the gate to the beach
meant the world was a possible apple;
that constant murmurs from overhead
signified the sky's name
had yet to be invented. True, there was
evidence to the contrary, mainly
those distant explosions

which often accompanied
the briny fragrance of evening
and anticipated sleep, and more
reports of an eleventh planet
cruising the limits of our system's cold
little room. But the shoreline
snored in the guestroom
down the hall, the hours opened
and closed with the same willful
consistency, and the days
turned into years at a speed suggested
only by the thin, metallic whine
I could sometimes hear
when the phone went dead: a foul-up
in the circuitry, or
the sonic afterglow
of the spoken word. Meanwhile,
her lapses of memory and taste grew beyond
my simple faith in the facts.
She stood less than ever on ceremony,
rising from confused siestas
seeing double and speaking
ill of the dead. One day
while I was out checking a shipment
of lenses for the small optical
equipment company I had owned
since childhood, she perceived
"unpleasant consequences"
at the bottom of a teacup
and tried to burn her diary, the sole
inside account of the intentions
and procedures of her visitants.
It took me ages to find her,

what with the smoke, the firemen
stumbling around, so I didn't wait
to break the news to her
about the sudden, utter displacement
of former times by these. We had dinner
afterward and discussed the matter
with the rational alertness
of people to whom adversity has revealed
the limits of having nothing
better to do. Then I poured more wine
and turned on the radio in time
to catch the rest of another
evening at the opera. The reception
was so good we could smell the ozone
when the orchestra attacked
beneath the shared high C
of lovers who were already pretty far
gone in whatever third act
was about to consume them both.

Here Everything Is Still Floating

for Nicanor Parra

I'm walking
through the mystery
and melancholy of
a street that isn't
a piece of my world
anymore, but a slope
animated by its own
grey lilt, a slow swirl
by the edge of the sea.
Here everything is still
floating in a continuous
aftermath of flood
conditions: a little
bayside café which smells
of old cooking, the people
inside who may or may not
be waiting for more.
I sit down near a window
and order coffee expensive
enough to be thick
and sweet. A woman
at the bar starts singing,
I plan to build
a sort of pyramid there
where we can spend
the rest of our days.
I think of my Uncle
August, the unhappy
inventor, whose denials

of the never seen led to
his sudden disappearance
in a coastal fog.
Recalling the confusion
and fear I felt the day
he waved goodbye,
I look out the window
and notice a cloud
shaped like a bird,
and a surprisingly soft
night feathering near.

From a Doorway

I stand in the doorway and explain
in a loud voice,
Here I am, ready to replace you!

I walk over to the warm tumble of covers,

knees weak
from traveling all night.
I am

startled by my nakedness
and the knowledge I am already breathing

my own ghost.

To steady myself, to make the transition
easier, I begin to become as I was.

I sit down and wait
for the trees in the window
to darken and join hands.

It never takes long.

Betty & John

Betty didn't answer and continued
building the bookshelf. Seeing her muscles
gather beneath her skirt, which looked so thin
it seemed to want to join her flesh forever,
John wondered if he could be growing deaf.
Betty got out an aluminum tool box.
John decided he would say no more.
Betty found a heavy screwdriver and started
to screw the first of many long metal struts
into the walls. John remembered nothing
was easy. Betty began to sweat from the effort,
so she took off all her clothes. John suspected
that even though he hadn't been born yesterday,
he might be somebody else. Betty stopped
for a moment to scratch her elbow, just as
John looked out the enormous bay window
and saw lots of birds flopping around
in a Victorian moonbath. Suddenly
Betty reached up and touched an antler of the deer-
head above the mantel. Water jetted
out of the trophy's mouth and nostrils into
a limestone basin revealed by a sliding
panel in the floor in front of the fireplace
and surrounded by a profusion of ferns and tall grass.
John sensed the proximity of strange animals
in underbrush that seemed to go on for miles.
Betty turned, saw him as if for the first time,
and moved toward him, her smile reflecting
an unmistakable intention. When she kissed him

John felt a cool wind blow through his body,
scattering dead leaves, and bearing
in a gust of rain the promise of things
starting over again. Betty kissed a man
she had never seen before. John knew
the weightlessness peculiar to anyone
about to flower into song.

Bonnard's Wife

Rodrigues observes, "There's a lot
of yellow in it," and Bonnard replies,
"You can't have too much," remembering
the light when she stepped from the bathtub,
and her reflection bleaching the blue
diagonals of tile she stood on
as she toweled one leg, then the other.
He sees her bend to examine
the humid blur of her left foot,
then close her eyes to the room's
dazzle and resume her careful strokes
of calf and thigh, taking her time
with a rapt casualness that stirs
and soothes him for a long moment's
luminous accord. And the dish
of peaches on the dressing table,
each weightless, each a setting sun
he knows won't disappear.

Putting It Mildly

A gust of tropical warmth
as he waded toward the house
through knee-high snow.
Later, lights out, a woman's
laughter in the heating system,
a baby crying as if
from the bottom of a well.
The wind honing the gables
turned into footsteps overhead.
He got out of bed, was half-
way to the door when he noticed
a face in the window's suddenly
illogical foliage and heard
a voice, matter of fact, putting it
mildly, *You'll pay for this.*

Going Away

She seemed to be waiting
for a signal or a message
telling her to move, perhaps
for good. She had a look
which said her life
was neither here nor there,
but where I'd never dream
of finding it. What
had happened? What would?
We had only to wish it, and it did
in the countryside we drove through,
where the houses all exploded
softly, as if in a theater
ten years before, or in time
with the histories
of neighbors who had come
from Germany. At night
in the mirror, we saw our faces
ripple and break apart
in flurries of light. Making love
blindfolded, our breath like paper
being torn, was what remained
after everything else
had been taken away.
I know what you mean, she said,
but it was never me.
What we were looking for was
that instant of seeing
someone before politeness,

kindness, or even the hope
of love takes over, a moment
we could recognize when it happened,
but which we could never anticipate
or recall. Both of us
must have believed, say, in music
or voices from the trees we stopped
to watch that afternoon.
But neither of us doubted
that the word you trust is always
ready to change sides, to enter
the heart like a blade you can't feel
until after you awaken.
*I know what you mean,
but the woman in this picture
keeps a balance I'd never stand for.
Besides, the shadow of a branch
has cut her face in half.*
Further talk of places
we had been, not very interesting
places, where the good thing was
you didn't have to speak
the language. And afterwards,
sending each other telegrams.
Here I am at last, hers read.
*The buildings are whiter
than I imagined.* Mine read
essentially the same.

What It Was Like There

1
I have no way of knowing
how often I have listened
to the wind in the curtains
and your voice from another room
as if I were the one missing.

When I get out of bed,
certain I have heard
footsteps, a door open or close,
cold air carries me
from one end of the house to the other.

2
The wind would rise and fall all night.
The refrigerator would hum in the kitchen.

Slowly it would grow light
over the black roofs of the city,

and he would watch
his folded hands take shape on his chest.

He would remember coming awake
out of a sensation of falling,

thinking of his life as a white tablecloth
shaken, gathered up, taken away.

Where You Were Going

He couldn't stop thinking of you.
He got in his car and drove
to your house. He stood at the door,
rang until you opened it.
When you asked him inside, he saw
the letters you were writing,
the newspapers open to reports
of starvation, the travel brochures.
He sat down in the green chair.
You sat down in the orange one,
just out of reach. You said
you could not get over your
astonishment, but that you would
try, that your thoughts were lost
and might or might not return
to the subject of both of you.
He thought of what he owned,
of how he would need none of it
where you were going.
You wondered what you looked like,
wanted to look at yourself,
but you kept looking at him
and spoke again, interrupting
the circle he had been repeating
with his fingernail on the worn
flannel of his trousers. You said
you had yet to discover
what others were like when
they were most themselves.

He thought you meant you didn't
have the calm necessary
to understand nuances—
tone of voice, light in a room.
Silence held you again.
You heard the rain start
and remembered the ocean.
Let's go to sleep now, he said,
while we can. We'll get up
early, in time to decide
what to take, when to leave,
by what means, in what direction,
not looking back, leaving
everything just as it is.

Preparations

He washes the lettuce
leaf by leaf,
hangs it above the sink
in a wire basket.
Sets the lamb chop
in a hot skillet,
mixes oil
and lemon juice
in a coffee cup.
And stooping to a shelf
beneath the counter,
reaches for a bottle
marked by faint
horizontal stripes of glue
that once backed a label.

He holds the bottle
up to the light,
squints into
an obliquely angled window
he can see
suspended in shadow,
a lucid aperture
the size of a postage stamp,
which frames, despite
its tilt and waver,
a single tree branch,
each leaf clear-
cut against the red dusk

that always happens
at this hour, dry
and cooling, to any
partisan of the vines'
hunched diligence.

When the cork,
slightly countersunk,
gives with a jolt
to the pull of his arm,
he hears behind him
a noise somewhere
between a footfall
and a fingersnap.
The echo vanishes
in a whiff of must,
tannin, and perhaps
that sage-laden field
along the estuary
whose shape he seeks
and whose name
he says aloud
whenever he comes across
a map of France.

He glances
at the blue smoke
near the ceiling,
at the salad curled
and shining in its bowl,
at the chop on the plate
leaking a thin seam
of butter and blood.

Then he sits down,
pours a little
of the wine into a glass
decorated with
a cat and a bird,
and holds the glass
away from himself, offering it
to whoever still watches
from beyond this slow
moment of no return.

Auras

1
Lose an arm and acquire
the arm's ghost, flesh resolved
to what it has become, alive
and more than alive,

like a friend
advancing out of the least
remarkable event toward you saying,
"Now I know what the case has been all along."

2
In the woods the smell of ashes,
the remains of a fire
blackened by rain
and shaped like a wheel.

Sunlight fanning through branches
of the oak from which an owl
suddenly unfolds,
part of the tree falling.

3
Afterward, nothing at first
but the familiar glow of skin
and bone. And the odor of clay, humid
forage for the reverse journey.

And silence broken by the drop of pebble
or rock. The tick of water moving rung by rung
down a face I saw with my fingers.
And a barely audible whistle calling me.

The Ribbons

I knock a few times, rattle the doorknob,
take a deep breath, and walk inside.
Here they are, my overdressed relatives.
They have been waiting for hours. The ghost
of a large poodle, my best friend in high school,
veers from my fingers, and suddenly the dinner
I have just enjoyed turns into a big mistake.
But it's always like this, I remember,
this silence, this heavy odor of lemons.
Okay, I say, look what I brought you,
and I let a burst of ribbons escape from my suitcase.
Each ribbon has the face of a bird on it,
with a secret message for anyone in the right
position to receive it. They untangle themselves
and slowly float up to the ceiling.
All this is supposed to be a surprise,
but everyone has already started circling
with glowing, lifted faces in a hushed chorus
of congratulation. Music gathers in the dining room.
A wind stirs the ribbons, twisting and untwisting them.
Now we begin hugging and kissing each other, ready to forget
everything for the way it used to be. A warm hand
massages the back of my neck. Another unbuttons my shirt.

The Summons

for Larry Raab

I always knew it would happen.
All those lucky stars crowding
the sky don't say anything, it's
pointless trying to count them,
and thinking about the future
is like trying to tell your fortune
with ice cubes. It's good the moon
changes signs so frequently
(every fifty-five hours),
it gives me time to verify
the wreck of the life
that used to be my life.
The mansion, the limousine, the dim-
witted bodyguard, the gorgeous
blond who lived quietly inside
a bottle—there are things
which vanish from memory,
but these aren't some of them.
By now the way out—what to do,
see, eat, expect—is getting nervous.
You must hurry, it says.
*You must think, or the chips
won't fall where they may.*
I pack a suitcase, convinced
I still have my wits about me,
a few tricks up my sleeve,
and if all else fails
my subtle wordlessness
under pressure. Out of breath,

The Ribbons

I knock a few times, rattle the doorknob,
take a deep breath, and walk inside.
Here they are, my overdressed relatives.
They have been waiting for hours. The ghost
of a large poodle, my best friend in high school,
veers from my fingers, and suddenly the dinner
I have just enjoyed turns into a big mistake.
But it's always like this, I remember,
this silence, this heavy odor of lemons.
Okay, I say, look what I brought you,
and I let a burst of ribbons escape from my suitcase.
Each ribbon has the face of a bird on it,
with a secret message for anyone in the right
position to receive it. They untangle themselves
and slowly float up to the ceiling.
All this is supposed to be a surprise,
but everyone has already started circling
with glowing, lifted faces in a hushed chorus
of congratulation. Music gathers in the dining room.
A wind stirs the ribbons, twisting and untwisting them.
Now we begin hugging and kissing each other, ready to forget
everything for the way it used to be. A warm hand
massages the back of my neck. Another unbuttons my shirt.

The Summons

for Larry Raab

I always knew it would happen.
All those lucky stars crowding
the sky don't say anything, it's
pointless trying to count them,
and thinking about the future
is like trying to tell your fortune
with ice cubes. It's good the moon
changes signs so frequently
(every fifty-five hours),
it gives me time to verify
the wreck of the life
that used to be my life.
The mansion, the limousine, the dim
witted bodyguard, the gorgeous
blond who lived quietly inside
a bottle—there are things
which vanish from memory,
but these aren't some of them.
By now the way out—what to do,
see, eat, expect—is getting nervous.
You must hurry, it says.
*You must think, or the chips
won't fall where they may.*
I pack a suitcase, convinced
I still have my wits about me,
a few tricks up my sleeve,
and if all else fails
my subtle wordlessness
under pressure. Out of breath,

I close my eyes to steady myself.
A room takes shape—tall windows
hidden by curtains the color
of fog, large couches clustered
like islands, men and women seated
around a felt-covered table
by the fireplace. One by one
they turn to me, and though
I don't remember their names
I join them, telling
an attentive waiter
I will take no further calls.
Soon there is only
the rustle of cellophane
when a new deck is opened
and the snap of the cards
as they reveal what they know.